The Incredible
Alexander
Graham Bell

by Juna Loch
illustrated by Don Dyen

Scott Foresman
is an imprint of

Glenview, Illinois • Boston, Massachusetts • Chandler, Arizona
Upper Saddle River, New Jersey

Illustrations by Don Dyen

ISBN 13: 978-0-328-51665-0
ISBN 10:   0-328-51665-1

2 3 4 5 6 7 8 9 10 V0N4 13 12 11 10

TABLE OF CONTENTS

Chapter 1
Can a Dog Talk?

At first glance, this narrative may appear as though it's about the invention of the telephone, but it's really about a great man who did wondrous things to help his fellow human beings. This is also a story of me, a dog. I am a Skye terrier, which is a handsome kind of dog. My master, Alexander Graham Bell, or Aleck, taught me to talk. Some people say this is only a myth, but you can trust me. Dogs don't prevaricate (that means to tell lies).

Now, before we get to the telephone, we have to go back to Scotland. This is where my master, Aleck Bell, was born. A precocious and inquisitive child, he was always interested in how things work.

My master was very interested in vibrations. There was a grand piano in his living room. Aleck spent most of his time looking inside the piano and fiddling around (no pun intended). He noticed that different strings would buzz when he played different notes. He tried to interest me in it too, but I am a dog and naturally more interested in activities like chasing rabbits.

Aleck was also curious about how our mouths let us talk. He even constructed an apparatus that was a model of the human mouth.

One day my master started moving my mouth, so that I made the sounds "Ow-ah-oo, Ga-ma-ma." He called in the family to witness.

Once again, my master moved my mouth so that I said, "Ow-ah-oo, Ga-ma-ma."

"The dog asked, 'How are you, Grandmama?'" my master said.

Here I must set the record straight. I don't want you getting the wrong idea. I was not really asking the ancient granny how she was feeling. Unlike human beings, dogs do not spend their days exchanging pleasantries and idle small talk.

My master made me make those sounds because he was interested in how the throat and mouth make human sounds. He wanted to put that knowledge to an important use: to teach deaf people how to speak. When he was only twenty-four years old, he got his chance. He arrived in Boston, Massachusetts, and took a job teaching deaf people, which, from then on, he always described as his life's work.

Chapter 2
Teaching the Deaf to Talk

To teach deaf children to talk, my master used a system his father had invented called Visible Speech.

If something is visible, it can be seen. Visible Speech showed you where to position your teeth and tongue to make any sound! My master and his father showed this system to professors at many colleges.

Now, my master Aleck thought that if hearing people could use Visible Speech, then deaf people could too.

He showed his deaf students how to make all the different sounds. He taught them to move their tongues to the back of their throats so they could make a *k* sound. He showed them how to open their mouths to say an *a* sound and how to put their tongues to the backs of their teeth to say *t*. There you have it, my least favorite word, *cat*. His students could not hear that they had done it right, but they could all say *cat*.

"What does this have to do with the telephone?" I hear you questioning. Well, this is part of the reason my master, Alexander Graham Bell, invented the telephone.

I want you to understand and appreciate my master the way I do. He did not think that the most important thing he ever did was to invent the telephone. He thought that teaching the deaf was more important.

Wanting to find an even better way to help his deaf students than using Visible Speech, my master built another human mouth. This time, the mouth measured the vibrations from speech. (Remember how interested he was in vibrations!)

Students could now measure the sounds they were making. My master also built a model of the human ear. He worked like a dog, and—you know me—I do not use that term lightly. But he still had questions that needed answers and problems that needed solutions.

Back in 1871, if you wanted to communicate with someone far away, you could only send a message along a wire using a kind of code on a machine called a telegraph.

By the 1870s, people knew that sound is made by vibration. If you strike an object in any way, it vibrates. The amount an object vibrates is called its "natural frequency." Some objects vibrate a lot, while other objects vibrate a little. But here's something amazing: if you put two objects that vibrate the same amount near each other and strike one, the other object will vibrate too! My master thought these vibrations might be the key to making a telephone.

How would this help Aleck make a telegraph that could send more than one message at a time? My master did an experiment, attaching thin pieces of metal, or reeds, with different vibrations to a telegraph. Each reed could carry one message.

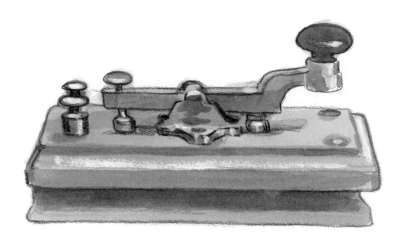

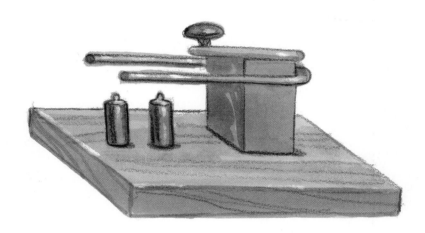

Could that message be picked up by another reed on the other end of the wire? My master thought so. He thought that the messages from the different reeds would travel together on the same wire. Each message would be picked up by a reed with the same natural frequency on the other end of the wire! My master called this idea the Harmonic Telegraph. *Harmonic* has to do with *harmony,* which means "together."

Chapter 3
Teaching Electricity to Talk

Now if my master Aleck had not experimented with his piano as a boy, he would not have known about vibrations. If he had not known about vibrations, he would not have tried to make the Harmonic Telegraph. And if he had not been working on the Harmonic Telegraph, he could not have made the mistake that led to the telephone.

It's all tied up together, you understand. And if my master Aleck had not been so interested in everything, he would not have starting thinking about a *speaking* telegraph!

"Do you know how the voice works, my dear dog?" my master asked me one cold March day.

"When a person talks," my master explained, "the sound is made by air. As you breathe air out forcibly, the air passes through a structure called the voice box. The voice box vibrates, pushing the air together and creating little waves of sound. These sound waves travel through the air until they reach an ear. There, they strike the thin skin of what's called your eardrum. The eardrum tells your brain what it hears. Then, you hear it! Isn't that wonderful?"

I nuzzled his hand. "If we could only make electricity talk!" he said. I didn't really understand; but then, these things are rather complicated for dogs, after all.

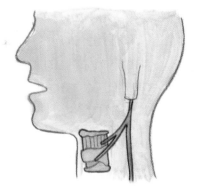

Air coursing through our voice box creates sound.

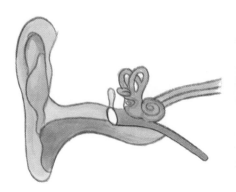

Sound waves reach the ear.

My master did not know how to make electricity speak. So he got a helper—a man named James Watson.

One day, they were working on the Harmonic Telegraph. "I want to make a speaking telegraph," my master told Watson.

"The voice isn't strong enough to carry very far," Watson replied thoughtfully. "How will we get it to move through the wires for miles across country?"

"The tiny eardrum is as thin as tissue paper," my master answered. "But it can move the bones of the inner ear. When that happens, we can hear." My master sighed. "If a tiny eardrum can move sound, surely we can find some way to do it too!"

I knew that a human voice could make me move to fetch a stick or run after a ball. And the human voice—even heard at a great distance—could certainly make me come in to dinner! If it could do all that, and more, maybe there was hope for my master and his experiments.

But hold on, because things are about to get really exciting. On June 2, a mistake allowed my master to see—well, what should I call it?—a miracle.

On that day, my master was in one room and Watson was in another, fiddling with the Harmonic Telegraph. I lay by his feet hoping he would scratch my head.

Suddenly, my master came flying out of the other room! He was breathless with excitement.

"What did you do, Watson?" he cried. "Wait—don't touch anything!"

We stared at him in amazement. When Watson had plucked at a telegraph reed, my master had *heard* its sound, rather than the coded signal it made. What's more, he knew exactly what it was he was hearing. If he had not been a musician, he would have missed it.

He also knew what it meant. Something as small as that plucked reed could carry a sound. That proved that the human voice could send sound over a wire too! By the following spring, Watson and my master had made a working telephone! He rushed to the Patent Office in Washington, D.C., to get a patent, which gives you ownership rights to an idea. He got there just a few hours before another scientist, Elisha Gray, who claimed to have invented the telephone too.

The telephone my master patented had two parts. There was a transmitter, which turns your voice into an electrical current. There was also a receiver. This receives the current and turns it into air waves. The transmitter was made of a small capsule filled with carbon grains. It was covered with a thin aluminum skin or membrane. When my master spoke into it, the membrane vibrated. When he spoke loudly, the grains of carbon moved close together. When he spoke softly, they were loose. Because the grains moved around, they created the different currents my master said he needed.

Inventing a telephone was exciting, but I, for one, was ready to take a break and chase cats. My master, however, couldn't seem to stop working. He was still interested in everything!

Three years after he invented the telephone, my master created a phone that worked by sending sound on beams of light! He called this a "photophone." Of course, dogs don't use phones, but it made humans very excited.

Now my master was famous and very rich. But he still spent his time and his money finding ways to better people's lives. Whenever people asked him what he did for work, he always said, "I'm a teacher of the deaf." Helen Keller, who was deaf and blind and couldn't speak, wrote a book and dedicated it to him. He was very proud. So was I, even though she didn't mention my name in the book.

Chapter 4
The Incredible Bell

In 2002, the U.S. Congress voted to give the credit for the first telephone to Antonio Meucci, an Italian-American who discovered the principle of the telephone in 1849 but who could not afford to patent his idea. Alexander Graham Bell received the first patent in 1876.

Bell still helped make the twentieth century incredible in many ways. He invented an elaborate device called an iron lung, which helps sick people breathe. He improved the phonograph, and he invented a machine called an audiometer to test hearing. Guess what? When we measure sound, we measure it in units called bels or decibels. They are named after Bell!

Bell remained, to the end, a man interested in everything. Along with inventing and teaching, he was also the first president of the National Geographic Society. He helped to make the magazine *National Geographic* into something colorful and fun for everyone to enjoy.

The Failure That Worked

In 1888, to the nation's horror, someone shot two bullets into President James Garfield. Amazingly, the President lived for weeks afterwards. A team of doctors tried to remove the bullets.

No one had x-rays back then, so no one knew where the bullets were. Alexander Graham Bell believed that he could help his President. Since the bullet was made of metal, he thought he could use a telephone rigged with magnetic coils to find it! He was sure the device would make a sound as it neared the bullet. He rushed down to Washington to try and save Garfield. His tests were inconclusive, though, and Garfield died a few weeks later.

Afterward, Bell learned that his wasn't the only new invention in the President's bedroom that day. The President had been lying on a new steel-springed mattress. The steel springs were what Bell's magnet had found!